AMAZING TRAINS

Passenger Trains

800

800

B&O

by Christina Leighton

BLASTOFF! READERS

BELLWETHER MEDIA • MINNEAPOLIS, MN

Note to Librarians, Teachers, and Parents:

Blastoff! Readers are carefully developed by literacy experts and combine standards-based content with developmentally appropriate text.

Level 1 provides the most support through repetition of high-frequency words, light text, predictable sentence patterns, and strong visual support.

Level 2 offers early readers a bit more challenge through varied simple sentences, increased text load, and less repetition of high-frequency words.

Level 3 advances early-fluent readers toward fluency through increased text and concept load, less reliance on visuals, longer sentences, and more literary language.

Level 4 builds reading stamina by providing more text per page, increased use of punctuation, greater variation in sentence patterns, and increasingly challenging vocabulary.

Level 5 encourages children to move from "learning to read" to "reading to learn" by providing even more text, varied writing styles, and less familiar topics.

Whichever book is right for your reader, Blastoff! Readers are the perfect books to build confidence and encourage a love of reading that will last a lifetime!

This edition first published in 2018 by Bellwether Media, Inc.

No part of this publication may be reproduced in whole or in part without written permission of the publisher. For information regarding permission, write to Bellwether Media, Inc., Attention: Permissions Department, 5357 Penn Avenue South, Minneapolis, MN 55419.

Library of Congress Cataloging-in-Publication Data

Names: Leighton, Christina, author.
Title: Passenger Trains / by Christina Leighton.
Description: Minneapolis, MN : Bellwether Media, Inc., [2018] | Series:
  Blastoff! Readers. Amazing Trains | Includes bibliographical references
  and index. | Audience: Age 5-8. | Audience: Grade K to 3.
Identifiers: LCCN 2016052936 (print) | LCCN 2017010870 (ebook) | ISBN
  9781626176737 (hardcover : alk. paper) | ISBN 9781681034034 (ebook)
Subjects: LCSH: Passenger trains–Juvenile literature.
Classification: LCC TF570 .L45 2018 (print) | LCC TF570 (ebook) | DDC
  625.2/3–dc23
LC record available at https://lccn.loc.gov/2016052936

Editor: Nathan Sommer   Designer: Lois Stanfield

Printed in the United States of America, North Mankato, MN.

Table of Contents

WHAT ARE PASSENGER TRAINS?

Passenger trains take people on long trips. These trains are found from coast to coast.

Passenger trains travel far and wide. Riders see pretty **scenery**!

THE GHAN EXPEDITION

stops: 5

days: 4

nights: 3

1

2

3

AUSTRALIA

route

4

5

distance: 1,851 miles (2,979 kilometers)

The Ghan, Australia

BUILT FOR PASSENGERS

Locomotives often pull passenger trains. The trains have many different **cars**.

cars

locomotive

People eat in dining cars. In **lounge** cars, they chat and play games.

dining car

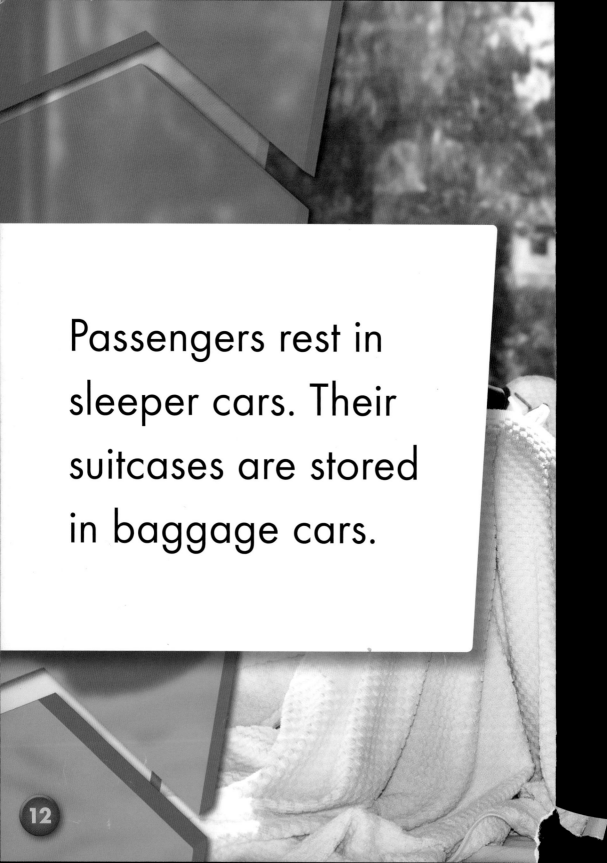

Passengers rest in sleeper cars. Their suitcases are stored in baggage cars.

sleeper car

FAR AND FUN TRAVEL

Passenger trains follow long tracks. They pass fields and mountains.

tracks

The trains often stop during the day. People can get off to **sightsee**.

sightseeing

At night, passenger trains do not stop. They ride through all weather!

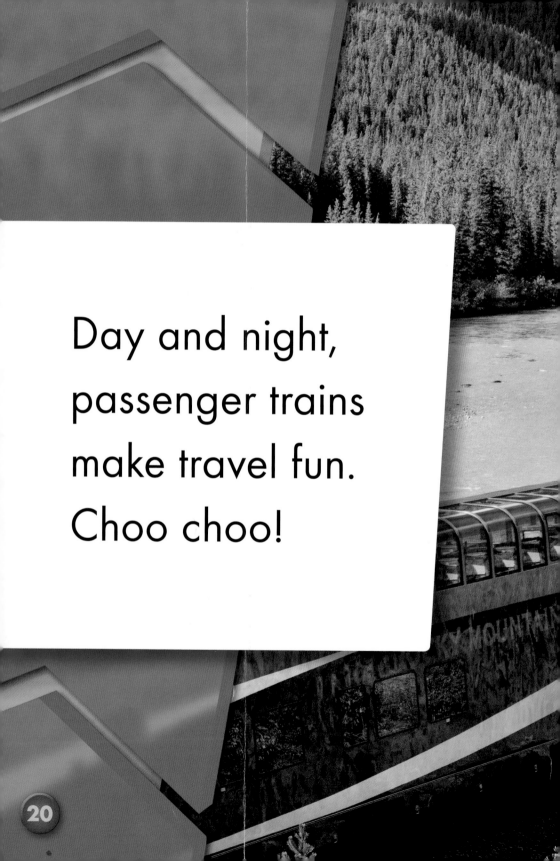

Day and night, passenger trains make travel fun. Choo choo!

Glossary

cars

vehicles pulled by a train

passenger

a person who rides a vehicle to get from one place to another

locomotives

vehicles with engines that pull train cars

scenery

outdoor views that are nice to look at

lounge

to pass the time and relax

sightsee

to see places of interest

To Learn More

AT THE LIBRARY

Clapper, Nikki Bruno. *Passenger Trains*. North Mankato, Minn.: Capstone Press, 2016.

Rosenbaum, Andria. *Trains Don't Sleep*. Boston, Mass.: Houghton Mifflin Harcourt, 2016.

Ryan, Phillip. *Passenger Trains*. New York, N.Y.: PowerKids Press, 2011.

ON THE WEB

Learning more about passenger trains is as easy as 1, 2, 3.

1. Go to www.factsurfer.com.

2. Enter "passenger trains" into the search box.

3. Click the "Surf" button and you will see a list of related web sites.

With factsurfer.com, finding more information is just a click away.

Index

The images in this book are reproduced through the courtesy of: Kenneth Sponsler, front cover; Scanrail1, pp. 2-3; Design Pics Inc/ Alamy, pp. 4-5, 6-7, 14-15; Sean Hsu, pp. 8-9; Jim West/ Alamy, pp. 10-11; Boaz Rottem/ Alamy, pp. 12-13; Tanwa Kankang, pp. 16-17; ralphradford, pp. 18-19; eye35/ Alamy, pp. 20-21; GE_4530, p. 22 (top left); Prasit Rodphan, p. 22 (top right); Albert Pego, p. 22 (center left); MELBA PHOTO AGENCY/ Alamy, p. 22 (center right); City of Angels, p. 22 (bottom left); RossHelen, p. 22 (bottom right).